A Note to Parents

DK READERS is a compelling program for beginning readers, designed in conjunction with leading literacy experts, including Dr. Linda Gambrell, Professor of Education at Clemson University. Dr. Gambrell has served as President of the National Reading Conference, the College Reading Association, and the International Reading Association.

Beautiful illustrations and superb full-color photographs combine with engaging, easy-to-read stories to offer a fresh approach to each subject in the series. Each DK READER is guaranteed to capture a child's interest while developing his or her reading skills, general knowledge, and love of reading.

The five levels of DK READERS are aimed at different reading abilities, enabling you to choose the books that are exactly right for your child:

Pre-level 1: Learning to read
Level 1: Beginning to read
Level 2: Beginning to read alone
Level 3: Reading alone
Level 4: Proficient readers

The "normal" age at which a child begins to read can be anywhere from three to eight years old. Adult participation through the lower levels is very helpful for providing encouragement, discussing storylines, and sounding out unfamiliar words.

No matter which level you select, you can be sure that you are helping your child learn to read, then read to learn!

LONDON, NEW YORK, MUNICH,
MELBOURNE, AND DELHI

For DK Publishing
Managing Art Editor Ron Stobbart
Managing Editor Catherine Saunders
Brand Manager Lisa Lanzarini
Publishing Manager Simon Beecroft
Category Publisher Alex Allan
Production Editor Marc Staples
Production Controller Rita Sinha
Reading Consultant Dr. Linda Gambrell

For Lucasfilm
Executive Editor J. W. Rinzler
Art Director Troy Alders
Keeper of the Holocron Leland Chee
Director of Publishing Carol Roeder

Designed and edited by Tall Tree Ltd
Designer Ed Simkins
Editor Jon Richards

First published in the United States in 2010
by DK Publishing
375 Hudson Street, New York, New York 10014

10 11 12 13 14 10 9 8 7 6 5 4 3 2 1

DK books are available at special discounts when purchased in bulk
for sales promotions, premiums, fund-raising, or educational use.
For details, contact:
DK Publishing Special Markets
375 Hudson Street
New York, New York 10014
SpecialSales@dk.com

A catalog record for this book is available
from the Library of Congress.

ISBN:978-0-7566-6690-3 (paperback)
ISBN: 978-0-7566-6878-5 (hardcover)

Printed and bound in China by L.Rex
Discover more at

www.dk.com

www.starwars.com

Contents

DK READERS

PROFICIENT
4
READERS

STAR WARS®

THE CLONE WARS™

Planets in Peril

Written by Bonnie Burton

Senate leader
Palpatine is Supreme Chancellor. He preaches peace, but secretly wants the war to continue.

Battle droids
The Separatists use battle droids as a cheap army. The standard battle droids can shoot weapons, pilot space ships, and drive tanks.

A galaxy divided

War rages throughout the galaxy! On one side are the forces of the Republic. Against them is the Separatist army, which is fighting to break away from the Republic's rule.

The Republic's army is controlled by the Senate, a group of elected representatives from all corners of the galaxy. The seat of the Senate is found on the city planet, Coruscant.

In battle, the Republic army is led by the Jedi who serve as its generals. They include Obi-Wan Kenobi and Anakin Skywalker.

Jedi generals have clone commanders who are often sent on dangerous missions. The commanders also pass on the generals' orders to the Republic's clone troopers.

The Separatist forces are led by Count Dooku and General Grievous. They report to a mysterious figure known as Darth Sidious. Together, they control an enormous army of droids.

From the center of the galaxy to its outermost reaches, many planets are suffering from the Clone Wars.

Clone troopers
Clone soldiers are identical. They are all clone copies, or clones, of the bounty hunter called Jango Fett.

Sith
Count Dooku used to be a Jedi Master, but he has turned evil. He wants to overthrow the Republic.

Clone troopers led by Jedi general Anakin Skywalker charge a group of battle droids.

Christophsis

Located in the Outer Rim of the galaxy, Christophsis is covered in enormous blue-green crystals.

Crystal power
The crystals on Christophsis are so large that the planet's skyscrapers are built around them.

These crystals are extremely valuable and can be used to power weapons, including a Jedi lightsaber. Over the years, the planet has attracted many different species who have built enormous cities on top of the massive crystals.

Droidekas
These destroyer droids have twin blasters and can fold into a wheel in order to roll into battle.

Separatist droids launch a massive attack on the planet Christophsis.

Christophsis has also attracted the attention of the Separatists. They want to use the crystals to power their weapons. Obi-Wan Kenobi and Anakin Skywalker lead a small team to deliver supplies, but become involved in an epic battle when the Separatists attack.

Republic forces repel the onslaught using heavy artillery, but are powerless in the face of another assault made under the blanket of a shield. Obi-Wan pretends to surrender in order to distract the Separatists long enough for Anakin to destroy the shield generator. Without the shield's protection, the Separatists are quickly defeated.

Kenobi
Obi-Wan is a high-ranking general in the Republic Army.

Anakin
Many of Anakin's tactics and plans on the battlefield are improvised.

Scrap dealers
The Jawas live by looking for scrap metal and broken droids, which they fix and sell. They wear long robes with hoods.

Hyperspace
Using the hyperspace routes enables spaceships to travel from one star system to another in very little time.

Tatooine

Tatooine is a desert planet. It is Anakin's homeworld and it is also home to the tiny Jawas and the enormous Hutts. Tatooine has twin suns and orbits near an important hyperspace route controlled by the Hutts. Both the Republic and the Separatists need to use this vital route, so they have to win the trust of the most powerful crime lord, Jabba the Hutt.

The Separatists try to trick Jabba by kidnapping his son, Rotta the Huttlet, and blaming the Jedi.

In order to win over Jabba, both sides promise to find little Rotta and return him safely.

Anakin and his Padawan, Ahsoka Tano, rescue Rotta, but the child is sick and must be returned quickly. Count Dooku sets a trap for them in the sand dunes outside Jabba's palace. The two Jedi trick the Count and manage to return Rotta to his father. Jabba sides with the Republic and lets them use the vital hyperspace route.

Jabba the Hutt
This crime lord is both feared and respected throughout the galaxy. His trust does not come easily, and with his son kidnapped, Jabba is not sure who to believe.

The towers of Jabba's palace rise above Tatooine's sand dunes.

Huttlet
Rotta may not know any words yet, but his gurgling and whining reveal his feelings. Jabba calls him "Punky Muffin."

9

Rugosa

The moon Rugosa was once covered in oceans. However, a plague released thousands of years ago dried up the water. Huge forests of coral were therefore uncovered, so Rugosa became known as the "Coral Moon." It is also chosen as the location for Yoda to meet the Toydarian King Katuunko. Yoda wants to ask the king to join the Republic's struggle—but the Separatists arrive first.

Yoda
Always patient, Yoda is the Grand Master of the Jedi Order. He may be small and seem frail, but he is more than a match for dozens of battle droids.

Fair play
King Katuunko is a shrewd but fair leader. He is willing to give both the Republic and the Separatists a fair hearing.

Landing craft
The Trade Federation, which works with the Separatists, uses these big ships to transport large numbers of battle droids, vehicles, and equipment.

Yoda and a small group of clone troopers break through the Separatist blockade using an escape pod. They crash on the moon's surface and all seems lost. The king is already in talks with the evil Asajj Ventress, kilometers away from Yoda. Not only that, an army of droids and tanks are on their way to stop the small Jedi Master from reaching the king. Yoda has walked into a trap—but he is not worried.

Escape pod
Escape pods are simple vehicles that only have enough fuel to travel to the nearest planet.

Yoda admires Rugosa's beautiful coral forests. Perhaps they can help the Jedi and his clone troopers by slowing down the Separatist droids.

Asajj Ventress
Ventress works with Count Dooku to defeat the Republic. She is a strong warrior and has defeated many Jedi.

Yoda and his clones battle through wave after wave of battle droids sent by Ventress. She wants to capture the Jedi Master to show King Katuunko just how weak the Republic really is. However, even though they are greatly outnumbered, Yoda shows the clone troopers how they can use their brains to outsmart their enemies.

The coral forests on Rugosa force the battle droids to attack on foot.

Assault tanks
Armored assault tanks use high-energy explosives. These tanks are dangerous, but they are also slow-moving.

Where the forests stop, the Separatists' tanks can be lured into narrow gorges— where they can be destroyed easily by a clone trooper using a single, well-placed rocket.

Eventually, Yoda and his clone troopers make it to King Katuunko at the meeting place, where Yoda scares off the evil Ventress.

Not even a pack of droidekas frightens Master Yoda.

As a result of Yoda's bravery and intelligence, King Katuunko is persuaded to join the Republic in its struggle against the Separatists and their droid army.

Asajj Ventress makes her escape using Count Dooku's own starship.

Super Battle Droids
Unlike normal battle droids, Super Battle Droids have dual lasers on their arms and stronger exteriors.

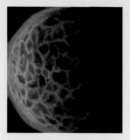

Cold moon
The surface of Rishi moon is very cold for more than half the year.

Rishi eels
These huge predators have four powerful jaws that they use to munch their prey.

Rishi moon

This remote and barren moon might not seem important, but it is close to the strategically vital planet of Kamino. Kamino is where the clone troopers are produced, which makes the moon very important. Set high on a cliff on Rishi moon is a Republic outpost that monitors the space around Kamino and can warn of any Separatist attacks.

The moon is also home to large Rishi eels. These eels live in tunnels, looking to make a meal out of any unwary clone trooper.

In a bold attack, the Separatists send a team of special commando droids to land on the moon. Using the element of surprise, the commando droids quickly take control of the Republic outpost.

Their aim is to keep the "all clear" signal transmitting so that the Republic is unaware that Separatist cruisers are approaching Kamino.

However, the droids had not realized how brave the clone troopers can be. A small group of soldiers sneaks back into the outpost. They destroy the base and, by stopping the "all clear" signal, warn the Republic that a Separatist attack is underway.

By destroying the outpost, the clone troopers are able to warn the Republic that Kamino is being attacked.

Commandos
These Special Ops droids have better combat skills than normal battle droids.

Long necks
Kaminoans are a thin species with long necks.

Swamp world
Home to large swamps and jungles, Rodia also has oceans and ice caps at its two poles.

Rodia

This hot jungle planet is located in the galaxy's Outer Rim and is home to the Rodians. The wildlife of Rodia can be far from friendly; many fearsome predators lurk in the planet's swamps and forests. To combat these beasts, the Rodians have become very good hunters over the years.

The Rodians build their cities on top of the swamps and forests that cover much of the planet's surface. Their cities are protected from the hot and humid environment by massive, clear domes.

Padmé
Padmé Amidala is the Senator from Naboo. She uses her position to negotiate for peace and an end to the Clone Wars.

The climate is kept comfortable and constant inside these enormous bubble-shaped structures.

Rodia is dependent on supplies from other planets in the galaxy. When pirates attack a number of supply convoys, the Rodians face starvation. Senator Padmé Amidala undertakes a hazardous journey through enemy space to help Rodia. She is desperate to enlist the help of an old family friend, Onaconda Farr, who is the leader of the Rodians.

Space yacht
This sleek, rocket-shaped vessel is Amidala's vehicle of choice. The unarmed ship is equipped with a powerful shield system, as well as escape pods.

Amidala's space yacht enters a Rodian city through one of the enormous gates in its dome.

Rodian senator
Senator Onaconda Farr is Padmé's old family friend.

Jar Jar Binks
Jar Jar may not be graceful, but he is always willing to help his friends. He often saves the day by being clumsy but effective.

C-3PO
This droid worries more than any other robot. When faced with a problem he prefers to panic, saying things like, "We're doomed."

It looks like Padmé has arrived too late. Onaconda says that he has already agreed to a deal with the Separatists. To make matters worse, battle droids capture Senator Amidala. The Separatist forces on Rodia are under the command of Viceroy Nute Gunray, who takes charge of his new prisoner.

Fortunately for Padmé, she is not alone on Rodia. Unfortunately for Padmé, she has brought C-3PO and Jar Jar Binks. These two struggle to make it out of the Rodian hangar where they have been waiting, but they manage to destroy a crab droid.

Then Jar Jar is mistaken for a Jedi Knight. Gunray and the Separatists panic when they hear that a Jedi might be on the planet.

Hiding in the swamps beneath the city, Jar Jar comes across a friendly local creature called a Kwazel Maw. This enormous animal proves very useful at smashing battle droids and Separatist ships. Before long, Nute Gunray and the Separatists have been defeated. The Viceroy is captured and is sent for trial on the planet of Coruscant, the capital of the Republic and the home of the Senate.

Nute Gunray
The Viceroy is high up on the Republic's most-wanted list of Separatist leaders.

Kwazel Maw
These large predators live in the oceans of Rodia. Their thick skin can repel battle droid blasters.

Senator Amidala is surprised to see battle droids on Rodia. Has she walked into a trap?

19

Vanqor

Located in the Outer Rim, the desolate planet of Vanqor hides large and deadly creatures. Beneath the planet's surface is a huge network of caves and caverns. Lurking in these dark places are terrifying beasts called gundarks, which wait for any unwary traveler to stumble along.

Obi-Wan and Anakin crash land on Vanqor while hunting Count Dooku. The two Jedi are lured into one of Vanqor's many caves—but Dooku brings down the cave's ceiling and traps them.

Cave system
The rocky surface of Vanqor is dotted with caves that lead into enormous underground systems. These labyrinths are perfect hiding places for gundarks.

Just when things couldn't get any worse, an angry gundark shows up, intent on making a meal out of the Jedi. Not only that, a cloud of poisonous gas starts seeping from the floor of the cave. Luckily for the Jedi, Anakin's Padawan, Ahsoka Tano, arrives just in time to rescue them.

Anakin later returns to the barren planet of Vanqor. He is hunting the young Boba Fett and a gang of bounty hunters who have taken a group of Republic officers hostage.

Gundarks
These creatures are one of the most vicious species in the galaxy. They are short-tempered and easily provoked.

Poison gas
Pockets of poisonous gas lie hidden beneath the surface of Vanqor. One crack can release a deadly choking cloud.

Florrum

The dry world of Florrum is the base of operations for Hondo Ohnaka and his band of pirates. The planet is covered with large deserts and rocky canyons.

Scattered around Florrum's deserts are the huge Doshar fields— which are dotted with large geysers that spew out jets of acid every few minutes. The only living creatures found in the Doshar fields are lumbering skalders.

To Ohnaka and his band of pirates, Florrum is the perfect place for their base of operations. No one visits the planet, so they can go about their business undisturbed. However, problems begin for the pirates when Anakin and Obi-Wan arrive on their hunt for Count Dooku.

Doshar fields
The Doshar fields are a deadly place to visit. The acid spewn out by the geysers is lethal enough to melt a clone trooper's armor.

Local wildlife
Skalders have tough hides that protect them from the acid geysers found in the Doshar fields.

Count Dooku has disappeared and the two Jedi believe that Ohnaka knows where the Count is. However, they don't suspect that the pirates could capture a Sith Lord and two Jedi. The Jedi are wrong— and are themselves captured!

Swoop bikes are perfect for traveling on Florrum. They can skim over the planet's rough terrain.

Pirate tanks
The pirates
have three
powerful hover
tanks. They use
these for any
heavy-duty
fighting.

Pirate droids
The pirates
have developed
their own
security system
by converting
normal droids
into armed
sentries.

With Anakin and
Obi-Wan taken
hostage, the Republic
has no choice but to
pay a ransom. Palpatine sends a
Senator and Jar Jar Binks with the
ransom to Florrum. However, some
of the pirates want to steal the
ransom, and shoot down the shuttle.

The Senator is killed in the
crash, leaving Jar Jar and the
troopers to cross Florrum's harsh
landscape. Using the thick-skinned
skalders for transport, the troopers
find the pirate base. Jar Jar captures
three pirate tanks single-handedly.

The small Republic force then attacks the pirate base in order to free the Jedi and capture Count Dooku.

The Separatist leader, however, manages to escape during the battle. With the pirates defeated, the Jedi leave without making arrests. They warn Hondo that Dooku is likely to return with a Separatist army. The Count will want revenge for being held hostage.

Bound together
Anakin and Obi-Wan are tied to Count Dooku during their time on Florrum. Neither the Jedi nor Dooku are happy with this arrangement.

Energy lines carry power across the desert to the pirate base. They also make the pirate base easy to find.

Maridun

The planet of Maridun is covered in rich grasslands and forests.

It has gone largely unnoticed for many years. It is therefore a refuge for beings who want to escape the violence of the Clone Wars. However, the Clone Wars are coming to this quiet planet.

Maridun is home to plenty of wildlife, but not all of it is friendly. Packs of large predators, called mastiff phalones, hunt in the long grass. These fierce creatures have razor-sharp claws and an enormous beak packed with large teeth.

Wildlife
The grasslands of Maridun are home to herds of corinathoths and large predators known as charnoqs.

Pack hunter
Mastiff phalones may have the head and talons of a bird, but they cannot fly. They use the long grass of Maridun to hide from any unwary prey.

Fleeing from a battle over the planet of Quell, a Republic frigate crashes onto the surface of Maridun. On board is an injured Anakin Skywalker, fellow Jedi Aayla Secura, and Anakin's Padawan, Ahsoka Tano.

Ahsoka and Aayla are forced to leave Anakin with the ship, with only Captain Rex to guard him. They have to go into the grasslands to find help for the injured Jedi. As night falls, Rex hears rustling in the long grass. Before he can react, a mastiff phalone leaps out and attacks. The captain is injured, but he manages to scare off the predator.

Air battle
The planet of Quell is the site of a ferocious battle between Republic battle cruisers and Separatist frigates. The battle does not end well for Republic forces.

Blue Jedi
Jedi Master Aayla Secura is a blue-skinned Twi'lek.

Lurmen
Some Lurmen
have the ability
to curl up into
a ball and
roll along
the ground.
They can cover
long distances
at great speed.

In the meantime, Aayla and Ahsoka come across a settlement of Lurmen. This peaceful race wants no part in the galactic conflict. The village elder, Tee Watt Kaa, is suspicious of the newcomers. He doesn't believe the Jedi keep the peace, but that they bring war, and asks them to leave. Ahsoka eventually persuades the Lurmen to help Anakin and a group of them set off to bring him back to the Lurmen village. However, Kaa's fears are realized when the Separatists arrive.

Defoliator
Two battle
droids survive a
Defoliator test,
as planned.

The Separatists have chosen Maridun to test out a new weapon called the Defoliator. This weapon destroys all animals and plants, but leaves machines and battle droids undamaged. Under the command of Lok Durd, the Separatists want to try out the Defoliator on the Lurmen's village.

The Jedi, clone troopers, and Lurmen set up a desperate defense, but they defeat the Separatists and destroy the Defoliator.

Lok Durd
Lok Durd is a Neimoidian. He specializes in the creation of new weapons and he is very proud of the Defoliator.

With Anakin recovered from his injuries, the three Jedi cut through the ranks of battle droids.

Cold-weather uniform
When the temperature drops below freezing, clone troopers have to wear specially designed armor to protect them from the cold.

Orto Plutonia

The icy world of Orto Plutonia was once thought to be deserted. The disappearance of clone troopers, however, indicates that something or someone might be living in the planet's frozen canyons and caves.

Anakin and Obi-Wan are sent to investigate, along with a squad of clone troopers and a group of politicians and guards from the nearby moon of Pantora.

The Talz ride large, catlike narglatches when they face the clone troopers.

The Pantorans claim Orto Plutonia as their own and do not like interference. Their leader, Chairman Chi Cho, is angry that someone has attacked the clone troopers. He demands that Anakin and Obi-Wan find out who is responsible and deal with them harshly.

The two Jedi discover that a species called the Talz are behind the attack on the troopers. The Talz do not like people being on their planet and they demand that everyone leave. It is up to Pantoran Senator Riyo Chuchi to negotiate peace before a battle begins.

Riyo Chuchi
Not long after negotiating a peace on Orto Plutonia, Senator Chuchi is taken hostage during a raid on the Senate by bounty hunters.

Freeco bike
This fast hover bike has a thick glass windshield to protect the driver from icy winds.

Naboo

Located close to the Outer Rim, Naboo has already seen its fair share of fighting. The planet was invaded by the Trade Federation even before the Clone Wars started. Naboo Senator Padmé Amidala is therefore even more determined to argue for peace during the Clone Wars.

Naboo is covered in thick forests and rolling grasslands. The humans of Naboo have built beautiful settlements, while its Gungans live in underwater cities.

Swampland
The dark and murky swamps of Naboo are home to the Gungans. They build their cities inside large spheres that can sit on the water or sink below the surface.

Battle droids ride hover bikes, called STAPs, over the grasslands of Naboo.

Trouble appears on the idyllic planet when Naboo soldiers discover and destroy a team of Separatist battle droids and a tactical droid. What are the Separatists doing back on Naboo? Meanwhile, a Gungan named Peppi Bow is shocked when her herd of shaak dies after drinking from a stream. It looks like the Separatists are up to no good. Obi-Wan, Anakin, and Ahsoka are sent to investigate.

Tactical droids are more intelligent than standard battle droids.

They uncover a plot by the sinister Doctor Nuvo Vindi to re-create the terrible Blue Shadow virus. If the Separatists are allowed to activate the virus, it would spell the end for hundreds of planets throughout the galaxy!

Shaak
These fat, plant-eating animals are raised on Naboo for their meat. They can also be used to ride about Naboo's plains.

Evil doctor
Doctor Vindi once worked for a powerful crime family. He has now turned his expertise to helping the Separatists.

Clone troopers open fire on Separatist battle droids in Vindi's secret underground base.

Blue beetle
This slug-beetle can be found only in one place—under the perlote tree in the eastern swamps of Naboo.

The Jedi have no idea where on Naboo Vindi's secret base might be. A lucky discovery by Jar Jar Binks points the way. A bright blue insect flies out of the captured tactical droid. The slug-beetle comes from only one part of Naboo. Arriving at Vindi's base, the Jedi and clone troopers quickly defeat the battle droids.

However, a single bomb of Blue Shadow virus explodes. Padmé, Ahsoka, and some of the clone troopers are trapped inside Vindi's base with the virus. They cannot open any doors as this would release the virus and destroy the entire planet of Naboo.

Their only hope is that Anakin and Obi-Wan can find an antidote to the virus before it kills them.

Blue Shadow
The deadly Blue Shadow virus was thought to have been destroyed, but Vindi has recreated it.

Reeksa plants
These meat-eating plants have spikes for teeth and are covered in deadly thorns.

Jaybo Hood
Young Jaybo Hood uses his skills as a droid tinkerer to reprogram battle droids to obey his commands. The droids now play relaxing music and wave cooling fans.

Iego

The antidote to the Blue Shadow virus is made from the root of the reeksa plant which can only be found on Iego. Many stories are told about this mysterious planet. People say it is a haunted place that no one can leave.

Anakin and Obi-Wan set out in Anakin's ship the *Twilight* to try and find the reeksa root. They land on Iego where they meet Jaybo Hood. Jaybo is a genius who has reprogrammed a small army of Separatist droids to serve him. He tells the Jedi where they can find the reeksa root, but it won't be easy.

They will have to avoid deadly xandu and the reeksa plants don't like having their roots dug up!

After a terrifying descent into a chasm and battles with xandu and angry reeksa plants, the two Jedi retrieve some of the root. When they try to leave, however, they find that a powerful security laser grid is blocking their path—they cannot escape.

The solution lies in Jaybo's battle droids. The Jedi send a squadron of Jaybo's vulture droids into the laser grid's control center. With the grid destroyed, the Jedi can fly back to Naboo and deliver the root in time to save Padmé, Ahsoka, and the others trapped inside Doctor Vindi's base.

Xandu
These batlike creatures have four wings, six eyes, and fangs. Anakin and Obi-Wan use one to fly down to where the reeksa plants grow.

Vulture droids
These fighter droids can turn their wings into legs to walk about.

Iego's spaceport, called Clifftop, sits atop of one of the planet's many jagged peaks.

Ryloth

Ryloth is a harsh and desolate place.
One side of the planet always faces
its sun and is baking hot. The other
side faces away from the sun and is
in permanent darkness and freezing
cold. Powerful winds blow across the
surface, carving deep gorges into the
dusty ground.

To survive on this planet is not
easy and many of Ryloth's animals,
such as the powerful gutkurrs, are
vicious predators. These two-legged
creatures have thick shells on their
backs that are covered in spikes.
They are always on the hunt for
their next meal.

The planet is populated by the Twi'leks. This graceful species has skin that comes in many colors.

At the ouset of the Clone Wars, the Separatists blockade and then invade Ryloth. They imprison the Twi'leks and position them as living shields around their bases. Under the command of Wat Tambor, the Separatists strip the planet, taking all of its valuable objects.

The Twi'leks appeal to the Republic for help. The Senate sends the Grand Army to re-take Ryloth, but first it has to break through a strong Separatist blockade around the planet.

Twi'leks
The most obvious features of Twi'leks are the two tentacles, called lekku, that grow out of their heads.

Wat Tambor
Wat Tambor comes from the planet Skako and has to wear a pressure suit to survive.

Jedi Master
Mace Windu is
one of the most
powerful Jedi.
He is second
only to Grand
Master Yoda.

AT-RT
All-Terrain
Recon
Transports are
difficult vehicles
to master.

Smashing through the
blockade, the Republic's army
lands on Ryloth. Under the
command of Mace Windu, it
heads toward the city of Lessu to
capture the Separatist leaders.

However, battle droids manage
to destroy many of the Republic's
AT-RTs and AT-TEs, and the clone
troopers suffer heavy losses.
Jedi Master Windu must turn to an
unexpected source for help.

Windu tracks down the freedom
fighter Cham Syndulla. The Jedi
needs all of his negotiating skills
to persuade the Twi'lek
to join the fight.

*The only way in or
out of Lessu is across
a plasma bridge.*

AT-TE
The All-Terrain Tactical Enforcer is a Republic assault walker equipped with laser cannons. The walker has six legs.

Together with the Twi'lek freedom fighters, Windu and the clone troopers storm Lessu. They have to be careful not to hurt any Twi'lek that Wat Tambor has put in front of the city. In the end, the Republic troops defeat the droids and Wat Tambor is captured.

Cham Syndulla
Ryloth's leading freedom fighter respects the Jedi but distrusts the Republic. He knows that the galaxy sees Ryloth mainly as a source for spice and Twi'lek slaves.

Geonosis

This rocky, barren planet is home to the insectlike Geonosians. They live in huge hives, which they have dug deep underground. Above ground, the surface of Geonosis is covered in towering spires and mountains.

At the start of the Clone Wars, the Geonosians side with the Separatists and build an enormous droid factory on the planet. The Republic invades and destroys the factory after a hard battle.

However, the Geonosians are not defeated. Under the command of Poggle the Lesser, they plan to build a new, bigger droid factory. The Republic is forced to invade again. This time, the Geonosians are better prepared for the Republic army.

Rocky world
Strong winds on the surface of Geonosis have formed tall, thin spires of rock.

Rebel leader
Poggle the Lesser is the leader of a large colony of Geonosians living in the planet's rocky spires.

They shoot down the Republic's gunships before they can land at the battle zone. With Jedi and clone troopers scattered across the planet, the fight looks lost. Thanks to the leadership of Anakin and Obi-Wan, however, the Jedi defeat the Geonosians and destroy the new droid factory.

The new droid factory is protected by an energy shield, which makes an air attack impossible.

Gunship
Clone troops fly into battle aboard Republic gunships. Each gunship is equipped with seven laser turrets, eight light, air-to-air rockets, and two missile launchers.

Duchess Satine
As the leader of Mandalore, Satine wants to keep her people neutral and out of the Clone Wars.

Rebel leader
Pre Vizsla wants to return the people of Mandalore to their historic warrior ways.

Mandalore

Mandalore is a planet devastated by war. Horrible battles throughout its history have left the planet barren and inhospitable. The people who now live on Mandalore have built enormous underground cities that are protected by metal domes.

Many Mandalorians have also chosen a peaceful existence, because of their planet's warlike past. A new terrorist group, however, is trying to undermine the planet's government and its leader, Duchess Satine. The Death Watch has launched a number of terrorist attacks on the rulers of Mandalore.

A Mandalorian shuttle craft flies over the barren surface of Mandalore to the domed city of Sundari.

Obi-Wan Kenobi is sent to investigate. He uncovers a plot involving the Separatists. They are trying to force the Republic to take over Mandalore to stop the Death Watch. This would anger the Mandalorians, who would turn against the Republic.

The trail leads Obi-Wan to Mandalore's nearby moon of Concordia. Deep within an old mine, he finds the Death Watch base. He also discovers that the group is arming itself in preparation for a revolution against Satine and the government.

Death Watch
Members of the Death Watch are elite soldiers who are equipped with jetpacks, rocket launchers, and assault blasters.

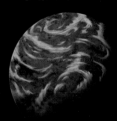

Concordia
Mandalore's moon is a forested world that has been devastated by decades of mining.

Massive city
At night, the lights of Coruscant glow from every part of the planet's surface.

Bounty hunter
Cad Bane is the deadliest mercenary in the galaxy. To Cad, it's the money that counts.

Coruscant

No planet is safe from the reach of the Separatists—not even Coruscant, center of the galaxy and home of the Galactic Senate. This planet is the capital of the Republic and its surface is covered with a single, enormous city.

However, Coruscant's political importance does not stop the Separatists from launching daring attacks on the Senate whose members think they are safe in the Senate building.

Cad Bane speeds away from the Senate building having set off a bomb to hide his escape.

Blue-skinned mercenary Cad Bane leads a group of bounty hunters to raid the Senate. They silence the Senate guards and put commando droids in their place dressed in the guards' armor. Next, they capture a group of Senators and demand the release of the gangster Ziro the Hutt. Anakin tries to stop the attack, but he does not have his lightsaber and is unable to defeat Bane. The bounty hunters escape the burning Senate after setting Ziro free.

Senate guards
The main task of the Senate guards is to protect the Senators, the Supreme Chancellor, and other members of the government.

Ziro the Hutt
Ziro is uncle to Jabba the Hutt. Even so, he still takes part in the plot to kidnap Jabba's son Rotta.

Glossary

battle droid
A soldier robot. Most of the Separatist army is made up of battle droids, also known as "clankers."

bounty hunter
Someone who hunts down and captures other people for money.

clone trooper
A soldier created to serve in the Republic army. All clone troopers are genetically identical.

freedom fighter
Someone who fights against a wicked government to win their freedom.

geyser
A jet of hot, boiling liquid that shoots out of the ground at regular intervals. The liquid is heated by hot rocks underground until it has enough pressure to shoot up to the surface.

hostage
A person who is taken prisoner and held for a ransom.

hyperspace
A region through which spacecraft pass when traveling faster than light.

inhospitable
Somewhere that is not very comfortable. An inhospitable landscape has features and conditions that are not good for life.

Jedi Knight
A member of the Jedi Order who has studied as a Padawan under a Jedi Master and who has passed the Jedi trials.

Jedi Master
A rank for Jedi Knights who have performed an exceptional deed or serve on the Jedi Council.

mercenary
A soldier who is not loyal to one side or the other, but fights for the money.

Padawan
A youngling who is chosen to serve an apprenticeship with a Jedi Knight or Master.

predator
An animal that hunts other animals to eat.

provoked
When something is made angry.

refuge
A safe place where someone can go to avoid trouble.

Senate
The government of the Republic, with representatives from all parts of the galaxy.

sentries
Soldiers who stand guard at the entrance to a building.

Separatist
Against the Republic; belonging to the Confederacy of Independent Systems.

species
A type of plant or animal. There are millions of different species, each adapted to suit the conditions it lives in.

terrain
The type of ground you travel over.